Memories and Miracles

By Tom Wright

Memories and Miracles
Copyright © 2004 and 2021 by Tom Wright.

All rights reserved. No part of this book may be reproduced or transmitted in any form or by any means, electronic or mechanical, including photocopying, recording or by any information storage and retrieval system, without the written permission of the author or publisher, except for the inclusion of brief quotations in a review or article, when credit to the book, publisher, and order information are included in the review or article.

First Printing
Library of Congress Cataloging-in-Publication Data
Wright, Tom;

    ISBN 0-0000000-0-X
    1. War stories — Vietnam
    2. Biography
    3. Religion

Dewey System — War: Vietnam

Second Printing
ISBN 978-1-954509-01-6

Unless otherwise indicated, Scripture quotations are from the HOLY BIBLE, NEW INTERNATIONAL VERSION (R). Copyright ©1973, 1978, 1984 by International Bible Society. Used by permission of Zondervan Publishing House. All Rights reserved.

Other Scripture quotations are from the New King James Version, Copyright 1979, 1980, 1982 by Thomas Nelson, Inc. Used by permission. All rights reserved.

Cover design by Juanita Smith
Text design by Debbie Patrick, debbiepatrick.com, Knoxville TN
Printed in the United States

Foreword

Memories and Miracles is no ordinary book. It is an honest account of a courageous man's memories of Vietnam. You must read it. You will be compelled by every page to read the next page. Tommy has recounted events and thoughts of the most misunderstood war in the history of the United States of America. Yet, Tommy did not misunderstand a vital truth in the midst of it all: God's miracles still happen.

Imagine being a young man on the other side of the world in a hostile territory called Vietnam. Imagine the daily dangers of battle being compared in your mind to the quiet and gentle surrounding of an East Tennessee home that is now far away. The longing for home would be tremendous. You can imagine how much pressure that would place on a yourng man's mind and spirit, but Tommy didn't imagine it, he lived it everyday he spent in Vietman.

Our collective appreciation as a nation ought to go to the men andn women who served in Vietnam. Our collective prayers should still be offered for families who through death gave up a precious loved one. As a nation we should re-visit our patriotism and generate a renewed heartfelt thanksgiving to all who selflessly and sacrificially served in Vietnam.

Tommy is a true patiot and a true soldier of the Lord. May the events he shares with you in Memories and Miracles bless you as much as they have me — and may all be to the glory of God.

Roy D. Graves
Pastor

Acknowledgements

I want to express my appreciation to the following individuals: my editor, Debbie Patrick, whom I know the Lord sent; my wife, Karla, her mother, Estelle, and my Pastor, Dr. Roy Graves, who together encouraged me every step of the way.

Dedication

This book was written as a testimony for my Lord and Saviour Jesus Christ.

It is dedicated to my daughters, Cheryl and Jessica, and my grandchildren, Nikita, Brittany, Samantha, Elizabeth, Marley, Lily and Hazel, and my great grandchildren, Kensley, Bentlee, Etazalynn, Maddox, Luxlee, Bryclee, and Cohen, as well as my stepsons, Karl and Shawn.

Memories and Miracles

From lightening bolts to Viet Cong bullets to hot steel, this book is a collection of memories and miracles that God has guided me through so I could share with others my testimony of God's saving grace.

Tom Wright

Memories and Miracles

Just one look at the lush green paradise we call east Tennessee, here in the Sweetwater valley, and you have to know that God blesses our lives. In fact, most of our lives are full of miracles, if we'll only take the time to pay attention, and listen. To prove my point, I'd like to share a few of the many miracles with which God has blessed me. In reading my stories, perhaps you will begin to see the miracles in your life, too.

Though others may argue that life begins at forty, and teens may believe it begins at 16 or 18, for me life began at 10. Everything happened when I was ten years old. At least, all the most important things. I met Jesus Christ that year when two women from a Baptist church came to our neighborhood to tell us Bible stories and teach us about God. I really enjoyed going to those meetings; they made the stories interesting by using an easel with stick-on pictures to portray the stories from the Bible. This method really "stuck" with me, as later in life I used the same technique when I taught the RA's (Royal Ambassadors) at church. The stories help make the concepts real, and the visual aid of pictures make the stories and truth of God's word stick in the heart.

When the ladies from the Baptist church stopped coming for classes, we neighborhood kids started our own church services. We held them in our basement at first, and then in an old school bus. We had singing; praying and preaching, one of my friends could really shout and preach. His dad was a preacher so I guess he received his messages from the Lord with some help from his dad. In all the years that have passed since that time, I've always enjoyed going to church and have continued to feel the presence of God in my life. My prayer is that as you read these stories you will look back through your own life and thank God for all your miracles. I also pray that if you haven't accepted Christ Jesus as your Savior, something in these stories of His love and power might prompt you to do that before it is everlastingly too late.

If My people, who are called by My name will humble themselves, and pray, and seek My face, and turn from their wicked ways, then I will hear from heaven, and will forgive their sin and heal their land.

2 Chronicles 7:14 NKJV

Memories and Miracles

Memories and Miracles

In 1933, congress formed the Tennessee Valley Authority or TVA, a government agency to manage the energy resources of the 49,000 square mile Tennessee River Basin, touching parts of seven different states. Throughout the 1940s, TVA built dams across the beautiful Tennessee River, flooding the valleys and creating lakes that never existed before. The power plants built with the dams helped the economy of the area, as did the cheap electricity, but I was a member of one of the many families who were bought out and moved by TVA in the process. Some families tried to fight the moves, but there was no stopping TVA. We tried to make the best of it, and bought our next house on a hill called "Happy Top."

The lakes formed by the dams were the best of TVA's influence. I grew up loving the wondrous beauty of Watts Bar Lake and was absolutely in love with fishing. My friends and my brother and I rode our bikes and motorcycles to the lake to fish and explore this wonderful new creation every chance we got. Harriman, Tennessee where we were raised was a very small town with little else to offer young boys yearning for excitement. Watts Bar Lake represented 39,000 acres of excitement just waiting for us to discover. Hilltops had become islands. Silos from abandoned farms peaked out like submarine sightings near the water's edge.

The TVA dams controlled the spring river floods that had been part of the life in east Tennessee for generations as well. Without the topsoil being washed away annually, the valley grew even more beautiful. It was a Huckleberry Finn type life. The only thing we loved as much as exploring the lake and surrounding area was baseball.

In the summer I spent nearly all of my time playing baseball. During the rest of the year, only school interrupted baseball. I loved the game, and so did all of my friends. We loved baseball so much that we even dreamed of baseball when we couldn't be playing. If we weren't playing or dreaming about baseball my brother and I watched the Bronx Bombers (now the New York Yankees) play on TV. We spent many hot afternoons cheering on our favorite team.

Those sweltering hot summer days also brought with them summer storms. There seemed to be so many bad thunder storms it was as if the clouds were playing bumper cars in the sky, with each collision creating yet another storm. The rain was good for the land, but the lightening that accompanied the storms was both dangerous and terrifying.

It was because of one of these electrifying storms that I became extremely afraid of them. First came a deafening clap of thunder, then lightning would split the sky with a fire-like zigzag pattern that too often found its landing somewhere very close to our hilltop house. Once it hit the roof of our house and shingles went flying into the air as if they had never been fastened down. That summer lightening hit many places right in our own neighborhood.

The tremendous force of a lightning strike knocked out a young girl who lived in the valley below us, and a house nearby was struck and burned by the extreme heat. That once gracious home proved to be little more than kindling for the powerfully dangerous lightning.

Two older boys I knew were picking blackberries when a storm came up suddenly and they ran for what they thought would be the safety of a huge oak tree. Lightning struck the tree killing one of the boys instantly and knocking the other unconscious. That tragedy had the whole neighborhood frightened and in an uproar. They began talking more about God and the Bible and how it is prophesied that God would take one and the other would be left. It was a scary time.

Memories and Miracles

*T**hen two men will be in the field; one will be taken, and the other left. Two women will be grinding at the mill; one will be taken, and the other left. Watch therefore; for you do not know what hour your Lord is coming.*

      Matthew 24:40, 41, 42 NKJV

Memories and Miracles

As I said, most of the important things in life began when I was 10, including my first miracle. It was that hot summer when a really bad storm came up and my mother, brother and I had taken our "storm position" on the living room couch. We always huddled together on the couch when a bad storm was brewing. Mom decided that she needed to go check the back porch to see if the rain was coming in, so we all went together to check.

My brother Jerry had a really good appetite – the kind we called a "hollow leg" and was always eating or looking for something to eat. He could make sandwich out of almost anything. I've seen him make a sandwich out of two pieces of bread with crackers in the middle. This time he took the opportunity to get a head of lettuce from the refrigerator as we passed. The three of us stayed together returning from the back porch. I was in front, with Mom and Jerry behind me. Then suddenly with supernatural force the impact of lightning hitting our house exploded in my ears. I went straight to the floor. I remember seeing a huge ball of fire pass in front of me and I crawled to the couch as fast as I could, thinking of it as a place of safety. I heard the sound of Mom's voice as she prayed that God would allow her to live to see her boys grow up. She and Jerry had both been hit by the lightning. It had come in through the wall and hit the bed just as we were walking by it. The heat from the lightning heated the springs on the bed to a temperature so hot that it actually burned the imprint into the mattress. Jerry must have instinctively thrown his arm around Mom to help protect her when the lightning struck and I suppose he took away a lot of the shock. The head of lettuce that had been in his hand now was in tiny pieces and had been blown all over the room like so much confetti. Mom had burns on her hands that looked like she had fallen against a stove, but there was no stove in the room. She had to spend the night in the hospital, but her prayers were answered. Thanks to God, she has been able to watch not only her boys grow up but also grandchildren and great grandchildren. We spent many more stormy days through the years sitting on that same couch praying that God would still the storm and that He would be gracious to us. He certainly has been that, and more.

Then He said, " I will make my goodness pass before you, and I will proclaim the name of the Lord before you. I will be gracious to whom I will be gracious, and I will have compassion on whom I will have compassion."

Exodus 33:19 NKJV

Memories and Miracles

My Dad and uncle owned a service station where I worked until I was old enough to get a "good" job. Maybe it was because I was part of the family, or maybe because of my age, but my pay at the station was only 20 dollars a week. I usually had to remind Dad to pay me even that much.

But Dad showed me love and care in so many other ways. He taught me the value of hard work, too. When I learned to drive, I paid $75 for a '55 Ford. I was so proud of that car. Dad spent many long hours and Saturday afternoons helping me fix it up and paint it. Never before had I felt so cool, or so full of confidence in my self than when I was sixteen, driving my own car and circling the "cool aid stands" – our slang for popular drive-in restaurants.

It was not the car, but my Dad that really helped give me that confidence. Now that I was a little older, he let me run the gas station by myself. It was a big responsibility for a 16-year-old, but that early sense of success helped me overcome a shy and quiet nature.

It was hard for me to start conversations with anyone, particularly outside my family. But working at the gas station helped me develop social skills that would help me a great deal in the near future.

I finally graduated from high school but at just 17, I was still too young to get a "real" job. By that time I already had a long history of helping dad work on cars, and I had learned to do a little welding too. In high school shop class I had learned even more about machines and engines and what made them work. God was paving the way, once again. At that time I had no idea how valuable all that knowledge would be, or how soon my survival would depend on it.

When I turned 18, a local hosiery mill hired me to work in the boarding room, where they stretched nylon hose over a hot metal form of a leg. The heat and steam would take a person's breath away. The pay was about a dollar-fifty an hour and I worked there until I was nineteen years old. By then, the Vietnam War was raging. What an impact it had on everything in my life. Lots of people were being drafted. It was the first war to be practically live on television, so even though it was halfway around the world, it seemed like it was right next-door. Sometimes it was all anyone seemed to talk about.

I was unable to get a better job or to even buy a car, because I was draft age. I was considered a bad risk. Who would hire me and take the time to train me knowing I could be drafted any day and they would never reap the benefit of my training? It was the same with buying a car. Draftees could too easily default on loans, or worse, never make it home. There were many men not coming home.

It seemed everyone my age was just waiting to get drafted. I felt like I was fighting a loosing battle right here at home, so why not really be fighting? I checked to see if any branch of the military except the Army was taking volunteers. The answer was no. I really didn't like the idea of the Army, figuring I would probably end up being in the infantry. The odds of surviving a tour of duty in the infantry were slim.

Someone told me that if you called the draft board and asked if you were on the list, they would draft you. Yet I felt I had nothing to loose, so I made the call and sure enough, was promptly drafted.

After basic training at Fort Jackson, South Carolina I took all the aptitude tests the Army gives to determine what you are best qualified to do. The officer giving the test asked about my interest in becoming a helicopter mechanic. I would love it! But I was still expecting the infantry, and guarded against getting excited about anything else.

When our orders were passed out, I wasn't sent to the infantry after all. I was going to be a helicopter mechanic. All that school training and hard work for my Dad had paid off. Yes, the Lord was really watching over me. He provided what I had not even dared to hope for: a more challenging and much safer assignment.

You will also declare a thing and it will be established for you; so light will shine on your ways.

Job 22:28 NKJV

One of the first things I received in the Army, (along with a military haircut and fatigues), was a New Testament from the Gideons. It was my constant companion, as I read it every time I had the chance. The other soldiers noticed. I was asked on numerous occasions if I really believed "that book." Each time I answered enthusiastically that I definitely did! It felt good to be a witness for Christ, but there were not many fellow believers during those early days.

Fortunately I had a true friend and brother in Christ in Mason Goodman, who at the time was Associate Pastor of Riverside Baptist Church in Harriman, Tennessee. At the time of this writing, he still serves as the dedicated Pastor at Riverside. Brother Mason wrote to me often while I was in Vietnam, to see how I was doing, and to encourage me. I want to take this opportunity to thank him for the uplifting letters he wrote. They helped me so much. I also want to thank all the wonderful men who donate their time and energies to do the work of the Gideons. There are soldiers all over the world whose lives are touched, enriched, and even saved through their work of making God's word available to all.

I am not ashamed of the Gospel, because it is the power of God for the salvation of everyone who believes...

        Romans 1:16 NIV

Memories and Miracles

My next assignment was helicopter maintenance school at Fort Rucker, Alabama. Frankly, I didn't learn much at the school other than some basic information about helicopters themselves, and how to safety wire parts. Safety wiring is a technique of looping a small wire around the bolts to insure that the wires are tightened securely into the threads of the bolts. This prevents the nuts from backing off, or loosening during the heavy vibration of flight. We learned to loop the wires from bolt to bolt in the same way to provide extra assurance that nuts and other parts, as well as the equipment they supported, would not shake loose under stress. But we didn't ever have the opportunity to work on real helicopters or engines during training. Still, all of the practice turned into reality real soon.

After I completed helicopter school, my orders came for Vietnam. I married my girlfriend six days before leaving. My head was still spinning as I left for Vietnam, a tiny nation half way around the world, to serve in a war I knew very little about.

It was pitch dark when we landed at the Bien Hoa airstrip. There had just been an enemy mortar attack on the area. Looking out the windows of the plane, we could see the jet pilots scrambling to their aircraft to prepare for counter attack. The reality set in at that moment. These were not games, and we were no longer in training. I was scared to death, not knowing what to expect next, and fearing the worst.

Memories and Miracles

When I finally stepped off the plane, the tropical heat and horrific smells enveloped my senses. This was different from anything I had ever experienced before, and I don't make that statement lightly. Having been raised in the South, I was quite familiar with the inner workings of an outhouse. But this stench was something else entirely. I'm sure it was the first exposure to outhouses for most of my fellow soldiers, and it was a real shock for them.

The absence of indoor plumbing was indignity enough, and quite an adjustment for us all, but there were new dangers to cope with as well. Sometimes we needed a buddy to be on the lookout just to be able to survive answering nature's call.

The rumor circulated that as a soldier sat down to relieve himself one day, he looked over at the next seat to see a cobra sticking his head up out of the hole. Now, whether the rumor was truth or fiction, it taught us all to carefully inspect the facilities prior to sitting down.

The outhouse consisted of a wooden shack built around a fifty-five gallon drum cut in half. Over the top of the drum halves, a shelf or seat was attached between the sides of the shack, with two ten-inch holes cut in it so the daily waste could be caught. All that smells bad enough. It was what the Army did with the daily waste that created an even more horrific smell, the one that assaulted me as I arrived.

The "daily collections" from the outhouses were mixed with diesel fuel or JP-4 jet fuel, and then burned. Without this safety precaution, the enemy would collect the waste and use it in their booby traps. The Viet Cong would dig pits, then place sharp stakes dipped in human waste into the bottom of the pits. When a soldier stepped or fell on the stakes, the waste could cause infection to set in more quickly, and be more deadly. No, this was no game. This was the reality of war.

Memories and Miracles

I was assigned to the 116th Assault Helicopter Company, a company that had been formed in July of 1965, and nicknamed The Hornets. The Hornets' first combat missions were in support of the first Infantry Division, as part of the 11th Combat Aviation Battalion based at Phu Loi. Phu Loi was 15 miles north of Saigon. It was near the Saigon River, and due east of Cu Chi about 10 miles.

The Hornets consisted of three platoons: the Stingers, the Wasps, and the Yellow Jackets. The Stingers were the gun ship platoon. In my opinion, they provide the best gun coverage in Vietnam. I never felt as safe with any other gun ships, as I did with the Stingers flying nearby. The Stingers flew UH-1C (Charlie Model) Huey helicopters. Their equipment consisted of 2.75 rocket pods, 7.62 mm electric-rive gatling gun (mini-gun) and two door gunners (crew chief and gunner), each with M-60 machine guns. If I compared the UH-1C to an automobile, it would be a two-door coupe.

Stinger Gunship

The Wasps and the Yellow Jackets were both lift platoons. They carried troops, supplies, equipment and served as a medevac. The lift platoons flew UH-1H Huey Helicopters called slicks. This meant there were no rocket pods or mini-guns hanging off the sides

27

of the aircraft. Except for our two M-60 machine guns the sides of the aircraft were clean or slick. Compared to an automobile the UH-1H would be a four-door sedan.

Wasp Slick

When I was growing up in Harriman, Tennessee, our biggest high school rivals were the Yellow Jackets in Kingston. It may seem funny now, but I was so very relieved to be assigned to the Wasps rather than the Yellow Jackets. I just couldn't imagine having to tell my friends at home that I had flown for the Yellow Jackets. Thankfully I was spared that discomfort. With the perspective that time gives; those thoughts seem so trivial considering the danger we were all in at that time. I even live in Kingston now, home of the "other" Yellow Jackets.

The Hornet pilots were great and I never flew with a bad pilot the whole time I was there. However, I did fly with some who took more chances than others. Some of them seemed to get a real thrill out of flying a little too close to the trees or taking a nose dive toward a herd of water buffalo, and sometimes I thought that the rotor blades would cut right into the nearby tree tops. I think that a lot of the chances they took were just for the shock they could evoke as a result of their pranks.

The pilots and I treated each other with the utmost mutual respect. One of the duties of the Crew Chief was to inform the pilots of any obstructions that might be encountered during take-off and landing maneuvers. I would always say, "Clear right or clear left, Sir". When we were entering and exiting the ship I would always open and close the pilot's door and slide the armor plate back on his seat. Some of the pilots and gunners would tell me to stop being so polite, because they weren't used to it and it made them feel a little uneasy. But that didn't matter; I never stopped showing my respect. I was proud to serve with the men of the 116th.

In November of 1966 the Hornets were moved to Cu Chi. I arrived there in February of 1970 at which time it was serving as the base camp for the 25th Infantry. The company area was great. We had a really nice chow hall and club, and we even had a swimming pool, compliments of frequent torrential rains. We did have a more traditional pool, too. Because the terrain in that area was so flat, when the heavy rains came the entire company area would be standing in water. You couldn't even tell where to step because the water would be so deep.

Company area at Cu Chi after a heavy rain

A few months later, July of 1970, we received orders to move to Chu Lai. It was the base for the 23rd Infantry Division. There we didn't have a club or even a chow hall and we sure didn't have

Memories and Miracles

a swimming pool. We did however have the South China Sea just a few hundred yards from my hootch. Having just moved from Cu Chi we weren't used to dealing with the sand and the new problems that it presented. The sand was everywhere, not only all over the ground, but also in our beds, in our clothes, our eyes, ears and mouth, but worst of all it was in the air. The sand made it next to impossible to keep our guns and ships clean. We landed our ship on the beach, once, and only once. Prior to that I had never heard of a salt air inspection, but the maintenance officer gave me a quick and memorable lesson. We had to clean the helicopter from top to bottom. I learned that the salt could have caused considerable damage to the frame of the helicopter. After that we avoided landing on the beach. I finished my tour and left for the states while the Hornets were still stationed at Chu Lai. The 116th later moved to Da Nang in October of 1971, and in December of 1971 the Hornets stood down. The men of the 116th were sent home to the United States or to other helicopter companies in Vietnam.

Back in Cu Chi, my orders placed me on the flight-line crew. Our job was to get the helicopters that had sustained only minor damage back in the war as soon as possible. Most of the maintenance we performed consisted of replacing parts, and making adjustments that could be done quickly. The young men I worked with taught me more about helicopter maintenance in just a few days than I had learned in three months of schooling. We were assigned to hootches, living quarters that were constructed of plywood and housed six to eight men. Hootches had vertical shutter-type openings on each side. These were also covered with plywood sheets, and hinged so they could be raised and propped open to allow airflow through the hootch. The floors were also made of plywood and stayed dusty all the time. Even with the panels on the sides propped open, the hootches smelled musty and damp all the time. One of the hootches I was assigned to was built directly over a bunker and had an opening in the floor, which would allow us to get into the bunker quickly in event of attack. The first time I saw the bunker, I was mortified to see that the entire floor of the bunker was covered with big black roaches about three inches long. I decided right then and there that they could have the bunker and I'd stick to the hootch. Later, when the first live mortar attack began I changed my mind and decided that the roaches might as well move over and make room.

Authors hootch at left and second platoon sign

No matter how bad life gets, it helps to see the humorous side of things. Take the wartime shower facilities for instance. The showers were fabricated using fifty-five gallon drum barrels placed up high, so that the sun would heat the water so that we could have warm showers. During the rainy season, we had heaters to warm the water. This was amusing to me because as a child, we didn't have indoor plumbing, either. We took baths on the back porch in a tub filled with water heated on the stove. One day Dad had the idea to put a barrel on the roof of the house, so that we could take a shower instead of a bath. When I saw the shower facilities it was like stepping back in time. I guess I had come full circle in a sense. The worst part about the showers in Vietnam was that sometimes you got all soaped up and then there was no water left to rinse the soap off. Then you would find yourself wiggling uncomfortably in bed that night because of the dried soap on your skin. It was next to impossible to get any sleep on those nights.

My first few days in Vietnam provided my first exposure to anyone using drugs. Having been raised in a very small town in addition to being quiet and shy, my life experience was very limited. Boy was I in for some real eye openers while in Vietnam! I was sitting on my bunk when a young soldier came in and fell on the floor in front of me and started kicking and going into a fit. I thought that he was dying. What I didn't understand was that he was under the influence of drugs. It frightened me, but also made me realize how blessed I was to have been raised by parents who had kept me away from drugs and the influence of people who used them. I have never used drugs or had any desire to do so. Moreover, I have always known without a doubt that my Mom would beat me half to death if she had any indication that I was using drugs, regardless of my size or age.

Memories and Miracles

*Train up a child in the way he should go,
And when he is old he will not depart from
it....*

Proverbs 22:6 NKJV

Memories and Miracles

I fell in love with flying after having worked on helicopters for about two months. We had just completed repairs to a helicopter and the test pilot was ready to take it up for a test flight. He asked if I wanted to go with him, and I jumped at the opportunity. I could hardly believe my luck to actually get to go up. Little did I know that the window of opportunity was just beginning to open wide. While we were in the air, he let go of the controls, turned to me and said, "You've got it."

What a rush of adrenaline! I could barely believe what was happening. Looking back, I'm sure I was shaking like a leaf in an autumn wind, palms sweating and throat dry. Honestly the only thing I really remember is the thrill I felt. It was love a first flight, and from that day on, I was hooked. I couldn't wait for another opportunity to fly.

The opportunity came much sooner than I expected. One morning a pilot came through the hootch looking for someone to fly gunner on the command and control helicopter. Tennessee, as you may know, is called the Volunteer state, so in true Tennessee tradition, I answered the call, even though I didn't know anything about the M-60 machine gun or what would be expected of me when I got up there.

I also dismissed from my mind the fact that I had promised my Dad that I wouldn't fly; I was excited about the opportunity. I flew for a year without telling my family about it because I knew that it would just cause them even more worry.

For me the first day out was great, the excitement was such a rush and the crew chief explained my duties and showed me how to use the gun. With time and experience I learned that the door gunner's job included firing at the enemy, giving cover fire for disembarking troops, relaying vital information to the rest of the crew, and serving as an extra pair of eyes for pilots and co-pilots. Door gunners were positioned on the sides of the helicopter and in most cases the doors were removed completely to allow more efficient operations of the guns, but it also left them completely open to enemy attack. The Crew Chief was positioned on the left side of the helicopter behind the AC the Aircraft Commander. The gunner was positioned on the right side of the helicopter behind the pilot, (usually a new guy).

Standard crewmember equipment consisted of a flame retardant Nomex flight suit, Nomex gloves and leather boots. The boots had to be leather because jungle boots would melt in a fire. Flight helmets and chicken plates (armor vests) completed the protective set. The Crew Chief and gunner manned M-60 machine guns with at least one thousand rounds of ammunition each.

The New Testament stayed in my pocket the entire time I was in Vietnam, except when I was reading it. I have kept one like it in my pocket ever since. My second day flying was a little more dangerous than the first. We picked up a group of Rangers who wanted to check out a landing zone (LZ). When we flew down low to look at a small grassy place a Viet Cong soldier jumped out and started shooting at us. We always flew with two gun ships that carried two gunners with M-60 machine guns. The ship was also equipped with rocket pods loaded with 2.75-rockets and mini guns that could shoot so fast that it looked like solid streams of fire flowing from the barrels.

The gun ships rolled in firing. Surely nothing could have survived that strike. However, the officers in charge weren't so sure so they called in an additional air strike. The jets rolled in and dropped napalm, a particularly powerful and deadly bomb, with a sticky chemical composition that burns to extremely high temperatures. The fire was so intense that every living thing in the area was burned to a crisp and there were several secondary explosions. When the fire died down we flew down to take a closer look. What we saw were the remains of two charred dead bodies. The odor that rose from them was a smell I can't possibly describe, but will never forget. Truly "war is hell."

But the Lord your God you shall fear; and He will deliver you from the hands of your enemies.

2 Kings 17:39 NKJV

Memories and Miracles

It's probably too late for me to remember everything I would really like to write. it has been over thirty-three years since Vietnam and I am fifty-three years old, but there were so many miracles God showed me, during the war as well as the rest of my life that I want to share with you.

Three of my grandparents passed away when I was just a toddler, so I don't remember much about them. I do have a very fond memory of the one grandparent I knew, Grandpa Settles. He was there the night I accepted Christ as my Savior. To this day I still remember that night vividly — I was twelve years old and it was in a small country church with a sawdust floor. I remember looking up and seeing the smile on Grandpa's face. I hope by writing this book I can leave a real record of what I did in life and in Vietnam to my children and grand children.

I guess one of the miracles is that I actually got to fly a helicopter. Many of the pilots wanted the crew chiefs to know how to fly in case they had to take over the controls. One particular time when we were flying in Laos and the commanding officer was flying my ship. He asked us if anyone could fly, and my gunner was quick to tell him that I could. He instructed that if he got shot, I was to pull him out of the way and to take over the controls. Thank the Lord it never came to that but, if it had I would have been ready. That's the way it is in the military, you must always be ready.

Another time I was flying to Da Nang and was having a great time flying along the coast of the South China Sea. It was still about an hour's flight to the base at Da Nang when it began to rain. Helicopters are equipped with windshield wipers but in truth they are useless. You still can't see a thing. I looked out to my right and saw two other ships flying close by so I decided it was time for someone with more experience to take over. I looked over at the pilot and he was sound asleep, so I woke him, gave up the controls and we made it there safe and sound.

My lack of any official flight training and limited hours of actual experience left me inept at landing a helicopter. The closest I ever came to making a good landing was within about three feet from the ground. We had just finished a mission and had picked up a load of troops going back to Chu Lai. I put a captain behind my gun and I flew us back. I made the radio call to the tower, that fact alone was enough to alert all in hearing distance of my voice of the fact that I was in control of the helicopter. As I mentioned earlier I am from Tennessee; a very small, some might even say, "hick" town in East Tennessee. So everyone in camp recognized my distinctively slow southern drawl.

In order to land I would have to fly along the runway and then make a right turn. I was about to make my turn, which in itself was a very awkward maneuver, the cyclic stick never seemed to grant as much control as a steering wheel. At just that moment I saw a giant C-130 airplane coming in my direction. The C-130 is capable of carrying troops as well as all their gear. You can imagine the intimidation factor to a helicopter in the way. I became so excited I pushed in the pedal, causing the helicopter to do a pirouette-type pedal turn in mid air. I'm not sure how the ship managed to stay together except that God was watching and protecting me as always. The turn was perfect and I took the ship within three feet of landing before the pilot took over. I was expecting the pilot to chew me out, but all he did was laugh and say, "You got excited, didn't you?"

Memories and Miracles

Whether you turn to the right or to the left, your ears will hear a voice behind you, saying, "This is the way, walk in it."

Isaiah 30:21 NIV

Memories and Miracles

Like I said, when I got to Vietnam I didn't know much about working on helicopters, but I learned fast. Working on the line crew we had to fix things that could be fixed fairly quickly. We could change rotor blades and tail rotors and make adjustments to them to eliminate vibrations. One day two gun ships came in from a mission and we were checking them for damage. They had been in quite a gunfight and were riddled with bullet holes. One of the pilots, who was known to be a little crazy and very fearless, had a bullet in the heel of his boot and he wanted a pair of pliers so he could pull out the bullet. He kept asking, "Will the ship fly, will it fly?" The pilot told us that he had to get back out there because the enemy had bunkers like Ramada Inns! He finally gave up on us and flew off to get back in the fight. When he came back just fine, I knew that God was watching over our whole company.

For the Lord your God is the one who goes with you to fight for you against your enemies to give you victory ...

Deuteronomy 20:4 NIV

When I first started flying, I flew Command and Control (C&C) missions. The purpose of the C&C ship was to fly around the Area of Operation (AO), and coordinate the operation. We had a radio console in the ship with four radios. I would call the flight tower every morning to get a radio check; to be sure they were all working properly. Usually when I finished the radio check, the maintenance Jeep would pull up full of men laughing at my thick southern accent overheard on the airwaves.

The C&C missions put us in the middle of combat every day. Our ship would pick up infantry officers, who would coordinate the movement of the troops on the ground. The AC and officers would decide the best location for an LZ and where gun coverage, artillery; and air strikes could be utilized most efficiently. Once the LZ had been located, we would fly low and fast into the LZ and drop a smoke grenade. The flight of helicopters would identify the color of smoke before landing so the enemy wouldn't draw the flight toward them.

On a mission near Cu Chi, we were flying around an area when our gun ships noticed some NVA clothes hanging in a tree. It appeared the enemy was somewhere nearby. So our gun ships started making rocket runs on the area, shooting in the general vicinity of the clothes. I was looking back, watching the second ship make his rocket run. As the rockets exploded I watched in horror as a red flash came back toward the gun ship, causing it to crash into the jungle. Three crew members were killed in action (KIA) and one miraculously survived. I never found out what the red flash was; it could have been a fragment off the rocket or ground fire.

Unloading troops in LZ

The C&C ship could fly around the troops and give all the support possible, but only God had control of the final outcome. It has been written, "some have entertained angels unawares." I believe I had the privilege to fly with many of them.

For He shall give His angels charge over you, to keep you in all your ways.

Psalms 91:11 NKJV

Memories and Miracles

Memories and Miracles

I knew God's angels were watching over me when my helicopter experienced an engine failure. That particular day I was flying as crew chief on another crewmember's helicopter. I knew my ship very well and took care of it like it was my prized 1955 Ford. All of the crew chiefs had to get up very early in the morning and go to the flight line, sometimes as early as one or two o'clock in the morning. We would pull a pre flight inspection on the ship and look at the logbook to see what kind of maintenance had been preformed earlier that night. My ship was equipped with a self-cleaning air intake filter, which meant I didn't have to clean any filters at the end of the day. The cleaning procedure for my helicopter consisted of the pilot keeping the ship running while I climbed on top of the ship and poured a couple of buckets of water through the engine to clean the carbon out.

I didn't notice that the crew chief on the ship I would be on that day had put filters in a self-cleaning intake. We were flying a mission out of a base camp on top of a mountain, and would be going to transport troops to another mountain landing zone. Usually when we did this, the landing zone was prepared for landing by hitting it with artillery or air strikes. Our gun ships would shoot the place up, then we would come in shooting our M-60's to keep the enemy down while we landed fast and got out fast.

The artillery had just stopped and we had been given the order to go. We took off and were heading toward the LZ when the ship kicked a couple of times and started falling like a rock. The crews of the other ships started hollering that there was smoke and fire coming out of the engine. The first thing I did was to check our altitude. We could auto rotate and land if we weren't too high, but in my opinion we were too high, so I said a quick prayer. I looked up at the instruments to check the status and noticed that the RPM light was flashing. The pilot had dropped the collective to try to auto rotate, as he had been trained. When I hollered at him to check the light he pulled back up on the collective and the engine started back up. The rest of the flight crews accompanied us as we flew back to base camp. The fact that they headed back with us also saved their lives, because there was an artillery round that blew up late in the LZ that probably would have killed a lot of us. The way I look at it, God used my engine failure to save us all.

You are my hiding place; you will protect me from trouble and surround me with songs of deliverance....

Psalm 32:7 NIV

Memories and Miracles

When we shut down the engine on a hill outside the base camp I checked out the engine and still didn't notice the filters. As the crew chief, it was my responsibility to stay with the helicopter until a larger ship (a Chinook) arrived to transport the damaged helicopter back to base. The pilot knew I didn't like the idea of staying on top of that mountain, so he said, "Just give me the word and we'll fly back to Chu Lai." We flew it all the way back only to be told when we landed that the engine was totally lost. That's when we found the filters; they had prevented the airflow required by the engine to perform properly. I was really angry at the crew chief. His mistake of putting the filters into the air intake had caused the engine failure and endangered our lives. However, I was thankful to God for watching over me for yet another day.

Memories and Miracles

Get rid of all bitterness, rage and anger, brawling and slander, along with every forms of malice. Be kind and compassionate to one another, forgiving each other, just as God in Christ forgave you.

Ephesians 4:31, 32 NIV

Memories and Miracles

As Crew Chief, one of my jobs was to maintain the logbook. The AC kept a record of the flight hours for the helicopter and I kept the maintenance records. During each refueling I logged the time and the amount of fuel we received. During the post flight inspections, I recorded all the necessary repairs that were identified during the inspection. The problems that would ground the aircraft were marked with a red X. A circled red X meant that the helicopter could be flown, but only for a limited flight time. The flight time was determined by what piece of equipment was malfunctioning. For instance, a fuel gauge malfunction would still allow a flight of two hours after refueling. A red X status could only be removed after all necessary repairs were made and the Technical Inspector (TI) had inspected the repairs, accepted them, and signed off in the logbook.

I can only recall one time while I was there that I missed the fact that the TI had not signed off in the logbook on a required repair. I had flown several long, exhausting days in a row, so I wasn't in top condition. I conducted the preflight inspections that day while I was still half asleep. The night before, I had written up a worn control rod (push pull tube) and the next morning during my pre-flight inspection I saw that the tube had been replaced. But I failed to notice that the TI had not signed off on the maintenance repairs in the logbook. I also missed the fact that the cotter pin had not been installed. The cotter pin kept the installation nuts from vibrating loose during flight.

Author catching up on log book between missions

We had flown for about four hours when the banging noise started. I told the AC we needed to land so that I could check to see what was causing the noise. He thought that it wasn't anything to worry about because all the instruments and controls were working fine. We had a Colonel onboard that flight, who thought he knew everything about a helicopter. He suggested that it was probably just one of the covers that the fasteners had come loose on, which would allow it to flap back and forth in the wind. Maybe. But finally I demanded that we land. When we shut down, I climbed on top to check. I found that the push pull tube had come loose and was hitting the short shaft. The short shaft was the piece of equipment that connected the engine and the transmission – quite a bit more serious than the Colonel's diagnosis of a loose cover.

We called for a maintenance crew to come and make the necessary repairs. After they replaced the tube with cotter pin this time, we were back in the air. Through the rest of the flight I kept imagining the trouble I was going to be in when we landed. I just knew that as soon as we landed I was going to get a terrible chewing out for missing the fact that the red X had not been signed off. After landing I went to the maintenance hanger and already the push pull tube was hanging on display. It was a reminder to all the maintenance personnel to check their work more carefully to ensure it was complete and correct. They had taken the chewing out that I had expected, and to my great relief no one even said a word to me about missing the sign off. When I had time to really realize the danger that we had avoided, I thanked God once again for protecting me and my crew from a probable fatal crash.

You are my hiding place; You shall preserve me from trouble; You shall surround me with songs of deliverance.

Psalm 32:7 NKJV

Memories and Miracles

There was always one helicopter that just seemed to be bad luck to fly; the one in our unit had the tail number 333. It had sustained several hard landings and engine failures. One day we received a call that it had suffered a hard landing in the jungle during a mission. The maintenance officer asked me and another flight line crew member if we would go with him to get the ship. We grabbed some tools and our flight helmets and flew to the ship with him. The ship was lying in the jungle with its landing gear crumbled underneath it. The pilot said he would start it up and hover it just far enough above the ground for us to get under it and take off the skids (landing gear). I guess the thought of the danger involved in being under a hovering ship brought a thrill of excitement to us, or maybe we were just too dumb to recognize the danger involved. It's just not smart working under a hovering helicopter that had just crashed. But we agreed, put on our helmets and plugged in communications so the pilot could tell us if there was any trouble. The pilot hovered the ship, while we removed the damaged skids. You've never seen two men work wrenches so fast. We dropped the skids off and the pilot flew it back without landing gear. It was the funniest looking ship I have ever seen. The pilot landed it on a stack of mattresses back at the base. That was the end of the adventure, except that the pilot got chewed out for flying the ship without landing gear. Still, in unusual situations you do what you have to do to get the job done. We did a lot of unusual things at times.

Memories and Miracles

Lost Ships

The war left many scars for many men, but I am convinced that God has given me grace to be able to deal with the agonies of the war without going crazy. I also feel that God has helped me go on with my life without having to endure many of the tragedies that some who served in combat went through. God watched over our Company in many ways.

In the fourteen months that I was there, our Company lost twelve men. That is a lot of American lives to be sure, but many other Companies lost that many soldiers in a single day. We once flew a mission in Cambodia that required moving troops all day, making numerous trips over the same area. It made the trips doubly dangerous because it makes the ships a more prominent and easily predictable target. I was flying on the Command and Control ship that day and we had just landed in an LZ when we heard a loud explosion. We heard a frantic cry from one of the pilots telling another pilot to "pull up, pull up!" The ship crashed, killing all four crew members. We flew over the crash site and immediately started receiving 51-caliber machine gun fire. That weapon had blown the downed ship apart, and three other ships were shot up badly.

Our gun ships moved in to cover, but were ordered to move away from the area. Our company commander had called in an air strike on the area. When the air strike was over, we moved troops in to secure the crash site. The troops captured the gun site and base camp. My ship had the grim job of landing at the crash site and dropping off body bags for the crew. A medevac helicopter arrived later and took the bodies to grave registration. We stopped by grave registration and the CO went in to give the needed information. You could see the pain on his face when he came out. It was a long flight home.

The army awarded survivors of such missions with medals; the crew of our helicopter received the Air medal with a V for valor (see attached documentation). We hadn't done anything on that mission that we hadn't done many times before, or that we wouldn't do again before we left, in order to protect each other. Years later, I have come to the conclusion that the Vietnam War was a political war, but we were there to protect each other. We would do some very reckless things to be sure everyone got out safely. We loved our country, but we were on foreign soil, half way around the world, in a war few of us understood. Our number one goal was for everyone to go home alive.

Memories and Miracles

Have I not commanded you? Be strong and of good courage; do not be afraid nor be dismayed, for the Lord your God is with you wherever you go.

Joshua 1:9 NKJV

Awards

Reason: For heroism while engaged in aerial flight in connection with military operations against a hostile force: These men distinguished themselves by exceptionally valorous actions while serving aboard the command and control helicopter during an air assault into an enemy stronghold in the Dog's Head Region of Cambodia. The lead element of the battalion came under intense automatic weapons fire from an enemy force defending a large well-fortified base camp. As they flew low over the contact area, they located the enemy positions and brought suppressive fire upon them. As the aircraft continued to make low level passes over the area, they directed accurate fire upon them, enabling friendly ground elements to maneuver effectively against the enemy positions. Their courageous actions led to the neutralization of the enemy positions and contributed greatly to the success of the mission, making it possible for the units on the ground to overrun the enemy base camp, destroy or capture its defenders, and capture sizeable quantities of enemy weapons, ammunitions, and supplies, with minimal friendly casualties. Their actions were in keeping with the highest traditions of the military service and reflect great credit upon themselves, their unit, and the United States Army.

I am the only person who benefits from these awards. They have never helped me get a job. In some cases, they probably kept me from getting a good job. I remember telling someone when I returned home from Vietnam that I had received thirty-five combat air medals. He told me I might be able to buy a cup of coffee with them. I didn't realize at the time how true that statement was. The public doesn't realize or appreciate the sacrifice combat veterans have made.

During the preparation of this book, I realized the combat veteran is not distinguished from the non-combat veteran. In a veterans benefit book I was surprised to see that the combat veteran and veterans that were not even in combat zones were listed together under just plain veterans. Only the wars served in are distinguished from each other. The benefits for the Vietnam in-country veteran were the same for the veterans who were stationed in the States or some other country.

Any Vietnam-era veteran is awarded the benefits regardless of whether or not they have had to experience the horror and fear of war. The only way for a combat veteran to get additional benefits for the stress of war is to prove that it has changed your life. Typically this means you must prove you can't handle everyday life because of the flashbacks.

I feel that God has provided for me, through faith and prayer, the power to overcome this stress. Someday maybe our nation's leaders will realize the life-changing experience combat is, regardless of how well you move on in life, and give the combat veteran the benefits he or she deserves. I know God will not forget my reward of everlasting life.

Memories and Miracles

I have fought the good fight, I have finished the race, I have kept the faith. Finally, there is laid up for me the crown of righteousness, which the Lord, the righteous Judge, will give to me on that Day; and not to me only, but also to all who have loved His appearing.

2 Timothy 4:7-8 NKJV

Memories and Miracles

On another mission while we were supporting a ground unit we received a call that we had lost one of our gun ships. We started making circles in the area, searching for the lost ship. Just as we came over a line of trees, we saw it scattered over an area the size of a football field. There were pieces of the ship everywhere. To our surprise, we saw three crew members lying side-by-side in the mud — waving at us! No one can tell me that God wasn't watching over those men. The pilot died from a broken neck, but considering the extent of the crash, the three surviving crew members were each walking miracles.

Memories and Miracles

Then no harm will befall you, no disaster will come near your tent. For he will command His angels concerning you to guard you in all your ways.

Psalms 91:10, 11 NIV

Memories and Miracles

Another day we had just finished a long mission of moving troops between LZ's when we received a call for an emergency search mission. A small observation helicopter (a Loach) had been shot down with three crew members onboard. One of the crew had escaped the VC and made it back to the base camp; however, he had been shot in the back. We loaded up ground troops and headed out for the site. Before we could make it to the LZ, it began to rain and was getting dark. As we landed, our rotor blades were hitting small trees. We dropped the troops off and flew back to the base camp to wait for news of the rest of the crew. Their bodies were found, but the VC had cut off their heads, arms and legs. These acts of malicious indifference and senseless cruelty caused each of us to hate the enemy even more.

Do not be afraid of those who kill the body but cannot kill the soul...

Matthew 10:28 NIV

Memories and Miracles

Once we were ordered to go into the mountains near Chu Lai and retrieve the bodies of a South Vietnam unit. They had been cut to pieces by enemy machine-gun fire. We picked up two US officers and supplies for the ground unit. The officers told us we would be dropping a net down through the jungle and picking up three bodies, and that we would receive the Vietnamese Medal of Honor if we could successfully complete the mission.

We flew up to the site and started our approach to the LZ. The two gun ships that were covering us shot rockets into the enemy machine gun position to keep them from firing at us while we attempted the recovery. We tried to hover three times, but on each attempt we lost power and started dropping. All the supplies plus two extra people onboard proved to be too much added weight. We finally decided to throw out the supplies. We flew over the ground troops and kicked out the supplies. On one of the flights over the troops, I saw a man standing near a big rock. I asked the pilot if any friendly troops were in the area. He said "no!" So I guess we inadvertently threw the supplies to the enemy. We never could get the ship to hover, and we couldn't get the two officers to get out either. I guess they intended to put themselves up for a medal. The mission was called off, and I never heard whether or not those troops got out.

Memories and Miracles

So he answered, "Do not fear, for those who are with us are more than those who are with them"...

2 Kings 6:16 NKJV

Sacrifice Or Suicide

The army made a lot of decisions regarding my life and most of them I didn't agree with, yet I followed the orders I was given because I felt it was my duty. The army took away two long years of my life and sent me into a war that very few people knew anything about, especially me. I got up early every morning and did my job fully believing it could be the last day of my life. This brings me to a mission I was picked for where my crew and I were going to be sacrificed to save others.

That morning our Sergeant came through my hooch and told me my helicopter had been picked for a special mission in Laos. They had picked my helicopter because it was new and very fast. The mission called for us to fly into Laos, drop down and perform a fake landing to draw the attention (and fire) of the enemy. While the enemy was occupied with us, the real landing team would be at a different LZ. The other helicopter would be carrying a long-range reconnaissance team. Just the thought of this mission almost scared me to death.

We weren't allowed to keep our weapons with us after a mission; we were required to lock them up in the armory at the end of the day. But we had a few weapons hidden, in case of an emergency. When I heard about the upcoming mission I went about digging up every gun I could find. I collected eleven guns in all, including a Thompson machine gun and a grease gun. The reason I wanted so many guns was because we had a hard time getting parts for our M-60's and more than once we had landed in an LZ only to have one or more of the guns to fail. I knew if we got shot down I would only be able to carry a couple.

The author at right with friend George Turk preparing for a mission

The night before the mission I couldn't sleep and I walked the floor praying fervently we would make it out alive. The sergeant came by once to check on me and asked me where I had gotten the 45-pistol I was carrying on my hip. I was lucky he didn't bust me and take the gun away, but he just left me with my thoughts.

The next day we sat on the airstrip for several hours waiting for the call to take off. My prayers were answered when headquarters called and said the mission had been called off. Several days later however, I flew a similar mission. But this time I hadn't had twenty-four hours to sit and think about it, and this time it was dark. We were called to provide a distraction to cover for the actual extraction of a Ranger unit. Our job was to draw the attention away from the extraction ship while it picked up the unit. As we flew over the area to draw the fire, my gunner and I looked at each other in total disbelief. We couldn't believe the mammoth size of the tracers that came by us. Since we didn't have any advance notice, we didn't have time to worry about this mission like the previously cancelled one. It did make me think about and appreciate a far greater sacrifice that happened many years before, when God sent his Son to die for my sins.

For God so loved the world that He gave His one and only son, that whoever believes in him shall not perish but have eternal life…

John 3:16 NIV

This is love: not that we loved God, but that He loved us and sent His Son as an atoning sacrifice for our sins…

1 John 4:10 NIV

Memories and Miracles

    There was one mission I flew that was a lot of fun at the time. It gave me an opportunity to do a lot of shooting and get rid of some frustrations. Called a spray mission, it was where we would spray the enemies' rice fields. It's a true saying that an army travels on its stomach. Without their main staple of rice, there was likely to be less fighting. We picked up two men who rigged the aircraft with a large tank of defoliant and a long boom with nozzles that stuck out the sides of the aircraft. The long boom made the helicopter look like a crop duster back in the United States. We didn't know anything about Agent Orange, or that it would be killing us many years later.

    We performed the spray mission with two helicopters loaded with the defoliant. We would have two Stinger gun ships in support. I don't know who picked the targets, but on this occasion our target was a very large village in the Northern part of South Vietnam. The area had lush green rice paddies bordered on the west side with high mountains. The mountains, while majestic and beautiful, also held their own secrets, because there were caves and spider holes (enemy fighting positions) facing the village. We were instructed that the area was a free fire zone, meaning anyone we saw could be shot. When we arrived at the site the village was totally deserted. If the occupants of the village were not already our enemies, they would be when we finished.

We sprayed the rice, shot the livestock and burned the village using white phosphorus grenades. Once we finished our carnage we flew back to the base and discovered we hadn't been totally alone in the area. One of the ships had two bullet holes in the tail section. I guess during all the shooting we were doing, we were also being shot at, but couldn't even hear the shooting. The crew and all the equipment were soaked with the spray. Now only time will tell if the war is still going to kill us many years later, as a result of those deadly chemicals.

Agent Orange was one of several defoliants (herbacides) containing trace amounts of a toxic contaminant called dioxin. Defoliants were used during the Vietnam War to kill vast areas of jungle growth. The name Agent Orange was derived from the orange strip on drums in which the herbicide was stored. (One of the pilots on this mission passed away in 2002 from what many believe was the result of exposure to Agent Orange.)

Memories and Miracles

*S*how me, O Lord, my life's end and the number of my days; let me know how fleeting is my life. You have made my days a mere handbreadth; the span of my years is as nothing before you. Each man's life is but a breath.

                        Psalm 39:4-5 NIV

Rockets And Mortars

I survived so many close calls with mortar and rocket attacks that I know God had to have been protecting me. For example, one of my duties as crew chief was to pull inspections on my helicopter before and after flights. These consisted of daily, twenty-five hour and one-hundred hour inspections. During one of the inspections I was on the flight line cleaning the fuel filter. I had finished cleaning the filter and was about to safety wire all the installation bolts, when I heard a loud explosion outside the perimeter wire. There was a rock quarry in the nearby village, so I thought they might be blasting rock. But then there were two more explosions and I looked up to see two clouds of black smoke about a hundred meters away from me. Everyone on the flight line began running for cover. While that's a natural impulse, it is really a bad idea, because the enemy would fire mortars two at a time and space them out and we could have run right under the next round. We ran to the barricade and God carried the next two over and past us.

Another close call was after we had stopped for lunch during a mission. Most of the time we would eat c-rations during the day, but occasionally we were invited to eat with the troops we were supporting. On this day we stopped at a fire support base and ate in their mess hall. We finished eating and had just taken off when we got the call that the mess hall had been hit with a mortar. I felt bad for those left behind, but had to chalk up another save for my guardian angel.

Memories and Miracles

*T*he angel of the Lord encamps all around those who fear Him, and delivers them.

Psalms 34:7 NKJV

Toward the end of my tour in Vietnam we received the call that our company was going to be moved to Quang Tri to support South Vietnamese troops going into Laos. The mission would be called Lam Son 719 and it would be one of the most frightening missions I ever encountered. Perhaps the main reason it was so frightening was because my service time had been completed and I should have been home already, but I had extended my tour forty-three days, so I could get out of the Army as soon as I left Vietnam. The mission could only be done with ARVN troops, since Congress had forbidden use of American troops in Cambodia and Laos after the Cambodian operation of 1970. I guess they didn't consider helicopter crews to be "American troops."

This relocation had us all worried because of the extremely high casualty rates other companies suffered after having been moved there. The North Vietnamese army had many weapons in Laos we hadn't encountered before. It wasn't unusual for a company to land four ships in an LZ and have three of them blown up. In our pre-mission meetings they told us about all the weapons we would need to look for. This didn't help our nerves any, because we knew that it was going to be really bad.

We moved our equipment to Quang Tri and they housed us in some old run down hootches next to the perimeter fence. After two days of preparation for the mission, the day arrived to start moving troops into Laos. I can only credit God for watching over our company again, because we completed our missions with no trouble at all. We took mortar fire in some of the landing zones, but we finished the mission and made it out with no injuries. My ship was ordered to take a load of water cans to a fire support base. As we were making our approach to the LZ, we were informed of a mortar attack just outside the base. The mortars were hitting just at the edge of the perimeter fence.

Ground forces estimated that there were five hundred enemy dead in the area. To this day I still don't understand how they determined that number. From what I could see there was nothing but desolation in every direction you looked. It is just beyond comprehension as to how they could possibly have determined how many dead bodies were strewn among the devastation we witnessed. Where the trees and brush had stood before the attacks, now lay only pieces, splintered and tossed in all directions interspersed with smoke and small fires here and there throughout the area.

The entire terrain around Laos appeared to be little more than bomb craters. The jungle that had once been thick and beautiful, with large trees and lush green underbrush now had been completely destroyed. Off in the distance we could see the Ho Chi Minh trail. It looked like a continuous row of bomb craters, created by our constant assault on the enemy's primary supply line.

We landed in the LZ and as quickly as possible I started unloading the water cans. As fast as I could reach and grab one I had it out of the ship and onto the ground. When I finished unloading all the water cans I jumped back into the ship, moved my gun back into position and suddenly noticed two wounded ARVN soldiers. They had boarded the ship without detection as I was unloading. I didn't know where they came from, and it really sent a fright through me to realize that someone was able to slip by me and onto the ship without me seeing them. We swiftly took off and flew the wounded to the aid station and waited for our next mission.

Memories and Miracles

Some of the other companies weren't as blessed. We heard "Maydays" over the radio several times that day. In one of the incidents, a ship was shot down and one of the pilots was running from the enemy on the ground. A cobra gun ship was sent to cover him, but was blown out of the sky. Another ship was sent and the same thing happened. Within fifteen minutes, five helicopters disappeared. The downed pilot kept running and finally hid in an enemy bunker all night. He was rescued the next day.

I can only begin to imagine what that might have been like to be running for my life, not knowing which way to turn, whether to move on ahead or to try to turn and retrace my steps. I'm sure that I would be expecting to run directly into the enemy at each turn in the path. Should I crawl around on my belly, or climb a tree, or try to bury myself in the underbrush? It's not hard to imagine that my heart would be beating so fast that surely anyone within a mile would be able to hear it and find me out, as if the sound would be as loud to them as it was in my own ears.

I know too, that if it had been me, the perspiration would be soaking my clothes and running into my eyes causing them to burn as though they were on fire, and my palms would be sweating. At the same time I was soaking wet from the sheer panic of the situation and the sweltering heat of the jungle, my mouth would be as dry as the desert. It scares me even to think of that pilot's situation. But I do know one additional thing: if I had been down behind enemy lines I would have been doing some very sincere praying for God's direction. I would have prayed that He would be my guide and that He would provide my protection through the night. He certainly did just that for that downed pilot.

After two days of moving troops we received orders that we could return to Chu Lai. We all gratefully celebrated our good fortune at getting out of that crazy place. We went into our hootches to get some much needed and well deserved sleep. Right after we had turned out the lights a bright light streaked over our heads followed by a loud blast. We all ran to the bunkers next to the hootches and the only thing you could hear in that bunker was the sound of people breathing hard, and your own heart beating loudly and rapidly in your chest. There were twelve 122-rockets that came over our heads. When the attack was over, we found the rockets had hit the hootches right behind us, killing twenty-two men within a hundred meters of us.

God once again had protected my company and me, but He wasn't finished yet. I had to stay an extra day in Quang Tri because my ship had mechanical trouble. I got very little sleep that night, wondering if we would receive another rocket attack. When I got back to the base the CO met me on the flight line to see if everything was all right.

The CO had flown with me into Laos. A week later we got the call to go back to Laos and pull the troops back out. I only had a few days left before my tour was over and I would be sent Stateside. The CO told me to stay back at Chu Lai since my tour of duty would soon be over. The rest of the company went back into the mountains and pulled the troops out. The ARVN troops were so scared that they threw down their weapons and when the ships landed, they would hang all over the ships in an effort to get away. Only about seven or eight of the small Vietnamese troops could be carried safely in each ship, so some of them had to be kicked off, as the ships were taking off. It was heartbreaking. Once again with God's hand guided our company and they made it out all right. The ship I would have been flying in had the glass blown out under the pilot's feet but none of the crew even got a scratch.

Even with all God's faithfulness to me, I contracted a case of short timers nerves after that mission. All I wanted to do or was able to think about was going home. I started having dreams about being back home. There was a popular country song out about that time, "Green Green Grass Of Home" and I started hearing it almost every day. After hearing it I would have dreams of running across the fresh mowed fields leading to my favorite fishing hole, only to awaken and discover I was still in Vietnam. I had logged over nine hundred combat hours and received thirty-five combat air medals. It seemed to me that there was nothing else I could achieve. The South Vietnamese were afraid to fight the war, and our politicians didn't want to win it, so all I wanted to do was get out alive and go home.

By April 1971, the last ARVN and American forces were withdrawn from Laos. The ARVNS had over fifteen hundred casualties. More than one hundred seventy-six Americans died, one hundred and twenty helicopters were shot down. The mission proved one thing, however; the only way the ARVNS could beat the NVA, was with a massive commitment of American air power to back them up and we had that power.

But I will rescue you on that day, declares the Lord; you will not be handed over to those you fear. I will save you; you will not fall by the sword but will escape with your life, because you trust in Me, declares the Lord.

Jeremiah 39:17,18 NIV

Memories and Miracles

There were some missions that sent fear surging through your veins just at the mention of the location. One such location was in the Mekong Delta, where it was common knowledge that the entire area was covered with booby traps. I still haven't figured out why the people in command would send men into a location like this where they knew the traps were set and a lot of men would be wounded or killed. It was as if they needed the injuries to prove what they already knew, that the area was booby-trapped.

On one such mission we had flown some troops into a location known as the pineapple fields. As soon as the troops started moving on the ground they started taking casualties from trip wires and all types of booby traps. In my opinion that is when I would have pulled everyone out and shot the place to pieces, but no, they had to keep moving around in that wretched place.

We had a call to drop some supplies off to the troops on the ground and we had instructions to watch for wires when we tried to land. Watching for wires is not an easy task when you're trying to watch the jungle for VC and the wind off the rotor blades is blowing the weeds all around. The grass there might grow to be three to four feet tall, and when that much grass started blowing around and bending over it became very distracting. About the time our skids touched the ground there was a loud explosion to our right front. We hadn't set off the explosion, but a young soldier had stepped on a booby trap. The troops hurriedly carried him to my ship. His right foot had been blown off at the ankle. They laid him in the ship and put his boot in the floor beside him. He was in so much shock he just lay there smoking a cigarette while his blood was blowing everywhere in the ship. We got him to the hospital, which was just a few minutes away, thank the Lord!

Memories and Miracles

Though I walk in the midst of trouble, You preserve my life; You stretch out your hand against the anger of my foes, with Your right hand You save me.

Psalm 138:7 NIV

Memories and Miracles

Memories and Miracles

One place I hated to go was a fire support base in the mountains. The troops there had serious drug and discipline problems. The enemy was everywhere around that place but the company stationed there didn't take them seriously. One day we dropped off some troops deep in the mountains and were following the river back to the fire support base. When we were almost there, we flew by an enemy base camp right out in the open. Our gun ships took great pleasure in blowing that place to pieces.

At another time, on a routine resupply mission one of our gunners was leaning out his door to look back when he was shot and killed within sight of the support base. He was a real quiet and very nice young man we called Jesus, and I'll always remember him because he had flown with me the day before and I had him laughing out loud several times with my southern drawl.

The support base was certainly no place to become nonchalant. It was completely destroyed one night when they had become too complacent. The enemy struck with a vengeance and very few survived the attack. I read an article on my flight home to the States about one of the survivors who played dead while an enemy soldier stole the watch off his arm. There was a South Vietnamese base located nearby, and the troops there were either afraid or were part of the attack, because they weren't wiped out. I believe God used those attacks to help us learn that even the easy missions must be approached very seriously.

Blessed is the man whom God corrects; so do not despise the discipline of the Almighty. For He wounds, but He also binds up; he injures, but His hands also heal.

Job 5:17, 18 NIV

Memories and Miracles

One of the things that I found the most frustrating and even infuriating about the Vietnam War was that the people in charge, those making the decisions and giving orders didn't seem to know what they were doing. They would order their men to fight for a hill or other strong point at the cost of many lives, only to have them hold the position for a short time, and then allow the enemy to take it back.

The company I was with was the 116th assault helicopter company. We were based at Cu Chi when we received orders that we were going to move up north to Chu Lai. We packed up and moved the entire company. The trip was six hundred nautical miles. We stopped several times for fuel, but one place always makes me laugh when I think about it.

Cam Ranh Bay was like stepping into another world. Right in the middle of that poor undeveloped country — which was mostly covered in jungle, mountains, and a few small farms — was this thoroughly modern city with paved streets with lights, up-to-date buildings and contemporary facilities. For a moment, it was like being back in the States in a big modern city, but at the same time it was almost surrealistic because it just seemed so out of place.

Right after our entire flight of helicopters landed a new Air Force jet, a C5 jumbo, landed. We had no idea it was about to land on its first flight into Vietnam. I was standing next to my ship checking it out after refueling when a Jeep with four Generals pulled up. They got out and started congratulating us for escorting the jet into the airstrip. We accepted the congratulations gratefully and never corrected their assumptions, but we had a few good laughs over it.

Flight of Hornets flying over Cu Chi in route to Chu Lai

When we arrived in Chu Lai we put our helicopters into containment positions once used by the Air Force. We got all our equipment unloaded and went to a meeting to be informed about a big upcoming mission. The mission was to retake an airstrip at Kham Duc that had been abandoned by the marines. Experts predicted that we could lose up to forty percent of our helicopters on this mission.

The morning of the mission was extremely tense. On our way into the strip radar picked up enemy aircraft leaving. The strip was prepared for our landing with a B52 air strike. As we were approaching, F4 jets were flying beside us. Our gun ships knocked out a thirty-caliber gun but we didn't loose a single ship on the first flight.

Retaking the airstrip at Kham Duc

The ground troops captured a few enemy troops but nothing on the large scale we had been told to expect. On our second flight in, my ship was just about to put down when the ground forces started screaming for us to pull up! The enemy had been tipped off that we were coming and had booby-trapped the runway before pulling out. My ship had been about to put down on a trip wire attached to mortars when the troops called us off. With a great deal of skill, our pilot stood the ship straight up and we avoided being blown to pieces.

The airstrip at Kham Duc was a frightening, eerie place. The remains of a C-130 airplane lying next to the runway was a reminder of the danger that surrounded us. Everyone on that plane had been killed during a troop withdrawal a couple of years earlier. It had been shot down while trying to take off. Our mission had been a success; we had captured the airstrip and a large number of weapons left behind by the enemy. The airstrip was used for a couple of weeks and then abandoned again. The last time I heard about the strip was when a Cobra pilot told us that while flying over the strip he had received ground fire. He said the enemy had dug a trench down the middle of the strip and had placed barrels in it, I guess to blow it up if we tried to use it again.

Even though I walk in the valley of the shadow of death, I will fear no evil, for you are with me; Your rod and Your staff, they comfort me.

Psalm 23:4 NIV

Flying In The Dark

Sometimes our lives seem to have no direction or meaning. I know my life has seemed this way many times, especially during the times I was laid off from work and felt there were no prospects for the future. I've come to realize that God is my pilot during these times as well as others, and I have to accept that and let God take control. I don't mean to just wait until hard times hit before turning to God, but that is how it seems to happen sometimes. I call these times flying in the dark, because I find I've been momentarily trying to go life alone without the guiding hands of our Lord Jesus Christ.

Let me give you an example of God guiding my helicopter crew and me during a night mission into the mountains of South Vietnam. As the crew chief of my helicopter, I flew with the ship every day that it flew. I knew almost all the fire support bases and the headings to take to get there. I sometimes used landmarks to remember how to get to many of the LZ's because I couldn't always look up at the instruments.

For the past several months we had been flying in the Mekong Delta where there was only one mountain and just a few hills. We had just moved to Chu Lai and there were mountains everywhere. I had flown a few missions into these mountains and I believe that made this particular mission even more frightening. I had enough knowledge of the area to know just how much danger those mountains presented.

We flew several missions at night. They were usually flair missions or "Chieu Hoi" missions. Flair missions were to light up the area around ground troops. The "Chieu Hoi" missions were missions where we flew around a given area playing several recorded tapes on eighteen large speakers. The messages and leaflets we threw out were used to encourage the enemy to "Chieu Hoy" which means give up. These night missions were flown with no lights and we weren't allowed to shoot back if fired upon. The enemy could come pretty close to hitting us just by shooting at the sound of our rotor blades. It's hard to explain how huge some of those tracers look when they streaked by us at night.

On this particular mission we had been ordered to fly into mountains that we had only seen once before, and that was during daylight hours. Our mission was to take a sight for an artillery piece to an LZ in the mountains. We weren't able to use any landing lights to find the LZ for fear of giving away the position of our ground troops as well as our own. The ground troops were going to use a strobe light to guide us in to their location. We took off on a heading that would take us close to their location. When we got close we knew mountains encircled us. The pilot put his trust in my gunner and me to help keep the ship away from the side of the mountains. We were to be extra eyes to help determine our exact location and the distance from the looming mountainsides. We had to trust the pilot's ability to fly the ship and the ground troops to guide us in to their location. Probably most of all, we put our trust in God to land us safely.

We finally got to the LZ and spotted the strobe light flashing far below. We tried to land twice, but the troops turned out the light and we lost their location. We couldn't fly around much because we knew the mountains were close and we didn't want to give away our position. The pilot finally told the ground troops that we were going to have to flash our landing light to land. After several minutes of deliberation they decided it was all right to flash the light. The pilot flashed the light and we all held our breath. In that faint flash of light I saw the troops and noticed that the air from the rotor blades was blowing their ponchos and equipment everywhere. One of the troops ran to the ship and I handed him the sight. We took off in short climbing circles trying to fly up and away from the mountains. Thanks to God's guiding hands we made it out all right and didn't give away anyone's position.

Memories and Miracles

I *will lead the blind by ways they have not known, along unfamiliar paths I will guide them; I will turn the darkness into light before them and make the rough places smooth. These are the things I will do; I will not forsake them.*

Isaiah 42:16 NIV

Jets Fly Under

On another mission in Cambodia our company was supporting the 25th infantry division. The ground troops were in heavy combat with the enemy and between the fighting and the heat they were badly in need of water. I was carrying a water jug on my helicopter that day and when we landed to pick up some troops I offered them my water. I gave them all I had and then got chewed out by the aircraft commander for giving away all the water.

I guess the pilot and I were having a bad day with the AC (aircraft commander), because we got chewed out twice that day. One of our gun ships had been shot up pretty severely and was forced to land in the jungle. We went in to retrieve the crew. A close friend of mine was flying gunner on the ship and he had been shot through the thigh and wrist. The pilot had a bullet in his boot. The command and control officers decided we needed an air strike on the area, so we called in two jets to shoot up the place. When the jets had finished making their runs we moved back in to survey the damage.

We were circling the target area, when I looked out my door and saw the two jets coming right at us out of the sun. The jets came so fast out of the glare of the sun that the pilot and I didn't have a chance to say anything. I know the Lord took control, because the jets dropped and flew under my ship. I believe if we had alerted the AC he would have dropped down right on top of the jets. The pilot and I took our verbal battering and went about our business, because we knew a miracle from God had kept us from being blown to pieces.

The Lord is my light and my salvation—whom shall I fear?"...

Psalms 27:1 NIV

Even to your old age and gray hairs I am He, I am He who will sustain you. I have made you and I will carry you; I will sustain you and I will rescue you.

Isaiah 46:4 NIV

Memories and Miracles

Loss of a Friend

All the training the army provides cannot prepare a person for the loss of a friend. The friend I lost was an officer. I met him through two other friends of mine who were also crew chiefs. I'll call him Captain Dean, which is not his real name. Out of respect for his family, I'd like to protect their privacy. We often drove Captain Dean to the officer's club and he would go in and get us something to eat. Because of racial tension in some of the local infantry units, our enlisted mess hall and club were off limits to us in order to prevent trouble. He told us to stand at attention and salute when he came out. This caused all the other enlisted people to stop and salute also. We would drive off and get a big laugh out of what just happened. Captain Dean lost his life through a freak accident.

The 116th always flew in formation. We had different formations for different situations as we were entering a LZ. I have a beautiful photograph of us flying in formation, which I have included in this book. The photo shows the shadows cast on the ground of our formation. Sometimes we would fly so close that you would think we were going to hit the helicopter in front. The strategy was that we had to put as many troops on the ground as fast as possible, and therefore had to have all the aircraft close together.

Shadows cast by formation of Hornet ships

One day we were flying in a straight formation, ready for landing on an airstrip. The helicopter in front of Captain Dean's ship flared up fast which caused Dean's ship to have to flare up to avoid a collision. Dean's tail boom hit the ground hard and caused the ship to crash. All the crew got out of the helicopter, but as Dean was moving away from the ship, the rotor blade came around and hit him killing him instantly. I will never forget the tears we shed at Dean's funeral, or the sight of his flight helmet lying on the table. But his smile and the laughs we had together will also be with me forever.

We cannot always prepare ourselves for death, but we can prepare ourselves for everlasting life. God tells us to clothe ourselves with his whole armor, that we may be able to stand against the wiles of the devil.

Memories and Miracles

For we do not wrestle against flesh and blood, but against principalities, against powers, against the rulers of the darkness of this age, against spiritual host of wickedness in the heavenly places. Therefore, take up the whole armor of God, that you may be able to withstand in the evil day, and having done all, to stand. Stand, therefore, having girded your waist with truth, and having put on the breastplate of righteousness, and having shod your feet with the preparation of the gospel of peace; Above all, taking the shield of faith, with which you will be able to quench all the fiery darts of the wicked one. And take the helmet of salvation, and the sword of the Spirit, which is the word of God;

Ephesians 6:12-17 NKJV

Christmas In A Combat Zone

My family was always very close when I was growing up. We sat down at the dinner table together every night, and I don't remember ever watching television while we ate. (There probably weren't but one or two programs on in those days anyway.) Christmas was always a very special time for my family, and the birth of Christ was clearly the reason for the season.

Christmas in Vietnam was a very confusing time for many of us in the service. We flew missions almost every day making it hard to tell what day of the week it was much less what time of the year. I started seeing the First Sergeant building something that I knew had to be for Christmas, but couldn't figure out what it was.

My friends and I started receiving Christmas presents from home, and the other men opened their gifts immediately. I found a small Christmas tree that I placed at the head of my bunk. I put my presents under the tree and waited for Christmas morning. Christmas finally arrived and we all sat and cried as I opened my presents.

We spent the remainder of the day on the flight line near our ships. We were on standby in case the enemy broke the holiday ceasefire. I finally realized what the First Sergeant was up to when I saw a Jeep coming down the runway shaped like a sleigh. What a sight! The "sleigh" was full of care packages from a church back in the States. The gifts made us feel a lot better about that day.

Then the angel said unto them, do not be afraid, for behold, I bring you good tidings of great joy, which will be to all people. For there is born this day in the city of David a Savior, who is Christ the Lord.

Luke 2:10-11 NKJV

Memories and Miracles

LZ'S and Bullet Holes

One of the missions we conducted almost daily was re-supplying and picking up troops in the jungle. The LZ was often little more than a few trees cut down to allow a small area to put the helicopter down. Sometimes we had to hover as low as we could and throw the supplies out, because there were too many tree stumps for us to land. If we were picking up troops in these small areas, my gunner and I would climb out on the landing gear and grab hold of the men one by one, pulling them up into the helicopter. Getting into these areas was very tricky, because we were trying to keep from hitting trees and crashing yet also trying to watch for the enemy at the same time.

On one of these missions we picked up a Colonel who was looking for a place to make an LZ for an upcoming mission. We were flying through a long valley in the jungle when we started receiving ground fire. From the unmistakable sound of the gunfire it was an AK-47. The funny thing about this war is that most of the time we had to get permission to shoot back. The Colonel onboard looked around and said, "I don't see why we can't shoot back." We flew back into the valley and shot the place up, and the ground fire stopped. The Colonel called in artillery on the area and we headed to a fire support base to check the ship for damage. When we landed we discovered a hole that was big enough to put your fist in. The bullet had gone in a few feet back on my side of the ship and level with my head. I knew that God had protected me and had other plans for my future.

The author waiting between missions

Memories and Miracles

The Lord will keep you from all harm – He will watch over your life; the Lord will watch over your coming and going both now and forevermore ...

Psalm 121:7-8 NIV

Memories and Miracles

Easter Morning

After almost fourteen months of combat flying, and being shot at by many different weapons — some of them with tracers the size of softballs — it was finally time to go home to the States. It seemed as if I had been in Vietnam for several years instead of several months. When the truck came to pick me up at the company area, the company commander came out and told me he would see me in Tennessee. When I got to the airfield two of my pilots were there and we had a good cry together. They said it seemed like I had always been in Vietnam. It was great to be going home, but very sad to leave the men who will be a part of my life forever.

The Flying Tiger Airline flew us back to Washington State. The army put us in barracks and treated us like we were new recruits. They screamed at us and rushed us to different locations. I woke up that morning to the sound of church bells ringing and realized it was Easter morning. It was 1971 and what a wonderful feeling flooded through me as I realized that God had brought me through the dangers, and now safely home.

After all the paperwork was done I was on my flight home. I had called my family to tell them I was back, but I couldn't tell them when I would be home. I was on Army standby flights so I didn't know when or if I would be able to get a flight out. I had seen some beautiful scenery while flying over the jungles of Vietnam and Cambodia, but nothing could compare to the beauty of the hills of East Tennessee. I finally made it to the airport in Knoxville, Tennessee and called home from there. It was about two hours before my family arrived to pick me up. I had waited fourteen months for this reunion and it finally happened!

Memories and Miracles

For you shall go out with joy, and be led out with peace; the mountains and the hills shall break forth into singing before you, and all the trees of the field shall clap their hands

Isaiah 55:12 NKJV

Job Hunting

The next few weeks were busy getting started on a new life. With money I sent home, my wife had bought furniture and appliances. We found a small three-bedroom house to rent, and later decided to buy it.

Rather than draw fifty-five dollars a week in unemployment, I decided to go back to work at the hosiery mill. At the end of two weeks I got my first paycheck — it was only sixty dollars. I wanted to sit down and cry. Instead, I told my boss I had to have something better, and he asked if I would like to work at a steel mill. If it paid more, I wanted it. He called his brother, who was personnel manager at the steel mill. After they talked, he came back and said, "They want you there tomorrow." I worked at the steel mill for ten years, ten years filled with miracles. It was also very hard work, physically and emotionally. While serving in Vietnam we had to medivac seventy men who had been burned in a rocket attack. It was a day filled with the smell of burned flesh. Every time I burned myself at the mill, it brought back memories of that horrible day.

The work at the steel mill was hot and very dangerous. But God's protection prevailed. One of the miracles that really stands out in my mind was when I was a caster in the steel mill, which meant I cast liquid steel into solid bars. The overhead crane operator would bring fifty tons of liquid steel over our heads and pour it into a box that would split it into three streams. On average, the steel was two-thousand nine-hundred degrees Fahrenheit. The steel would pour into three water-cooled molds, and come out the bottom of the molds as a solid bar. It's perfectly alright to pour water on hot steel but if hot steel is poured on water, it will blow up.

We had a system of continuously pouring the steel by a method of piggy-backing the ladles of steel. To piggyback, we used two cranes, the first crane would hook up to the empty ladle and the second crane would be waiting with an additional full fifty tons of hot steel. When the first ladle was empty the crane operator would move the ladle around and back away from the casting tower. As soon as the first crane was out of the way, the second one would have to come and follow the same steps as the first. The procedure had to be done within a few minutes or the steel would cool enough to cause it to stop flowing. This time the second crane came in too fast and couldn't stop. The ladle came to a sudden stop, and the hot liquid steel splashed out. The crew I worked with was standing directly under the ladle. We didn't have time to run and the steel splashed right at our feet. To our amazement God had prevented us from getting even the slightest burns. We ran out of the flames without a scratch.

But whoever listens to me will live in safety and be at ease, without fear of harm.

Proverbs 1:33 NIV

Memories and Miracles

Raising A Family

In 1973 our first child was born, and we named her Cheryl Mae. She weighed nine pounds and was 23 inches long, and was a perfectly beautiful baby. Maybe because she was so long, though, her feet and legs were misshapen and bowed. The Lord led us to a great doctor, who placed casts on her legs all the way up to her hips. She was just a baby and the casts caused her great discomfort and frightened her when he first put them on. I can still hear them banging together when she was sleeping. It broke my heart to hear her struggle, but I knew it would benefit her in the long run. The casts had to be replaced two or three times, but her legs and feet are straight and beautiful today.

We belonged to Riverside Baptist Church where I took on the job of teaching a young boys Sunday School Class. This led me to helping and then leading the Royal Ambassadors (RA's). I spent every weekend possible with those boys, as if they were my own. They taught me a lot, but most of the time I wasn't sure if I was getting through to them. But over the years, several of them have called and thanked me for my time and guidance. "The fruits of the harvest and the rewards far outweigh the material price we pay." I say this because I really didn't know if there would be a spiritual harvest among these young people. In addition, most of the time during the years I was teaching RA's, I barely had the money for gas to pick them up. Yet I drove several miles out of the way several times a week to pick them up and return them safely home. There were several times I felt down and defeated because I couldn't support my family the way I wanted to. Proverbs 11:28 (NIV) says, "Whoever trusts in his riches will fall, but the righteous will thrive like a green leaf." I know that God was leading me to help these young people and He has repaid me many times over for the efforts and energies I put into helping them.

Memories and Miracles

Command those who are rich in this present world not to be arrogant nor to put their hope in wealth, which is so uncertain, but to put their hope in God, who richly provides us with everything for our enjoyment. Command them to do good, to be rich in goods deeds, and to be generous and willing to share. In this way they will lay up treasure for themselves as a firm foundation for the coming age, so that they may take hold of the life that is truly life ...

1 Timothy 6:17-19 NIV

Jessica

Our second daughter was born in 1976. Officially, I was still working at the steel mill, but I had been laid off for a couple of months before Jessica was born. After Jessica was born, the hospital asked me how I planned to pay the bill. I said, "My bill! I have insurance." But the hospital said I didn't have insurance, because I had been laid off. I was back to work by then, so I talked to the union president to find out what was causing the confusion. We had a meeting with the company and they apologized for the error and paid the bill. God really does supply our every need.

A couple of months later we found out that Jessica, too, needed casts on her legs. I don't know if it the condition was inherited or if it was a side effect from Agent Orange that I was exposed to while I was in Vietnam. Whatever the cause, God was the cure. Through prayer and the knowledge of skilled doctors, Cheryl and Jessica both have perfect legs today.

For me, the late seventies and early eighties were filled with worry and sorrow. There were frequent lay-offs from the steel mill, and no other jobs in the county, yet every time I was down to my last unemployment check God would get me back to work. In 1981 my father had a massive heart attack and died. With his death I lost a very important person in my life. The sudden shock of his death devastated my family and me. I truly love my brother for being able to help our Mother make all the funeral arrangements. I was unable to be of help myself.

Before the army and Vietnam, I had never experienced the loss of a loved one. I remember trying to wash the blood and smell of death out of my helicopter, with little success. I remember being behind my gun looking at the body bags containing American men lying on the floor of my helicopter. I wondered who was in the bags and thought of the pain their families would soon go through. When my Dad passed away I realized that pain.

Even though I know my Dad believed that God sent His only Son to die on the cross for our sins, I still wondered if I had witnessed enough to my Dad and my family. It always seems to me that the hardest people to witness to are our loved ones and close family members.

I remember one deer season after Dad had passed away. During hard times I had sold my hunting rifle so I decided to use Dad's old gun. It was in pretty bad shape, but I shot it several times at close range and decided if a deer came close enough, I could hit it. Sure enough, a big buck come by at less than a hundred yards but I missed it four times. I remember laughing and telling myself I couldn't wait to tell Dad how bad his gun shot. Someday I'll get that opportunity.

At this very moment, I ask you stop reading and take the time to pray and witness to family members. Don't wait until it is too late.

For I am persuaded that nether death nor life, nor angels nor principalities nor powers, nor things present nor things to come, nor height nor depth, nor any other created thing, shall be able to separate us from the love of God which is in Christ Jesus our Lord

Romans 8:38-39 NKJV

Memories and Miracles

I was still in shock about my father's death several weeks afterwards, when my oldest daughter Cheryl came into the house holding her head. She had been swinging in a home made tire swing. Her hair had somehow gotten caught in the rope of the swing. It was a quirky accident. When she moved her hand I saw a place the size of my fist where the hair had been ripped from her scalp. Panicked at her pain, I just couldn't believe God was putting all these problems on me at once. Cheryl wouldn't let me see the place on her head anymore; she kept her hair pulled into a sideways ponytail until it grew back out. After I had time to calm down and think about what had happened, I realized God had been watching over her far better than I gave Him credit for. If her hair hadn't pulled out, it would have broken her neck.

Memories and Miracles

Do not be anxious about anything, but in everything, by prayer and petition, with thanksgiving, present your requests to God. And the peace of God, which transcends all understanding, will guard your hearts and minds in Christ Jesus.

Philippians 4:6, 7 NIV

Memories and Miracles

We all need a place where we can go or a hobby to help us relax and calm down from the fast pace of everyday life. My hobbies are hunting, fishing and gardening. I spend a great deal of time in a tree stand waiting on a deer, but I love it. Some of my friends will pass the time by reading — but not me, I don't want to miss a thing. I take in all the beauty. I sit and try to imagine why a  certain tree is bent the way it is, and how old it is. Then I wonder who used to walk or drive down that old grown up road in front of me. I watch the squirrels and birds searching for and hiding their food. To me it is fascinating. Sometimes life's worries try to creep up on me, but I push them out of my mind and enjoy God's wonderful creation. I love planting a garden and raising my own vegetables and flowers. Recently I built a small water garden, complete with waterfall, fountain, and goldfish. It produces a wonderfully calming effect; sometimes I just sit and listen to the bubbling sound of the water and enjoy the beauty. It's a true saying that life is neither a practice run nor a dress rehearsal, so I encourage everyone to take every possible opportunity to stop and enjoy all the beautiful things that God has created.

For by Him all things were created that are in heaven and that are on earth, visible and invisible, whether thrones or dominions or principalities or powers. All things were created through Him and for Him.

Colossians 1:16 NKJV

Hunting

Even though my father worked six days a week, ten hours a day, he always found the time to take my brother and me hunting and fishing. We always went to church on Sundays but sometime later in the day we also went hunting or fishing. It was the only time we could all go. The first few times we went squirrel hunting, Jerry and I took BB guns. Dad showed us how and where to shoot and how to be very safe. Those were some very special times together, because we were a very close family.

Memories and Miracles

Teach them to your children, talking about them when you sit at home and when you walk along the road, when you lie down and when you get up.

Deuteronomy 11:19 NIV

Memories and Miracles

    I have always thought of myself as a very safe hunter, but something happened once when I was older that changed the way I look at safety. Jerry and I were hunting near where my Dad worked. We had hunted in this area many times and we were after anything that was in season. Earlier in the day we had jumped some quail and we were walking through a field trying to jump them up again. We were just walking in the middle of the field when a covey of quail flew up. As I turned to shoot, my single shot shotgun went off. The hammer had slipped from my thumb with enough force to fire the shell. I had been turning in the direction of where Jerry was standing. Horrified, I was afraid to look at Jerry; I was sure I had shot him. When I did look, he was staring back at me in disbelief. Thanks to God's guiding hands he had not been hit. I never used that gun much after that miraculous day and we didn't tell our parents how careless I had been.

    Jerry and I first hunted deer when he was out of the Navy and I was home from the Army. He was an avid reader and always reading books and magazines. He subscribed to Outdoor Life magazine and it was there he got the idea to enter all three of us in a draw hunt on one of the wildlife management areas near our home. There were usually only three or four hunts in this area each year, and we got drawn for the first one. We went to the area and camped out in the campground. We didn't have any formal camping equipment; just blankets and a campfire. We almost froze to death, but Jerry killed a nice six-point buck, and Dad made sure we had plenty of camping equipment for future hunts.

My time in a deer stand is very special for me. I've made many decisions in my life while surrounded by the wooded beauty God created. I make it a point to start every hunt when I get to my stand by saying a prayer of thanks for the forest, and ask for protection for anyone who might be hunting with me and for myself. I remember one time I went to my stand to bow hunt one afternoon. I had climbed into the stand and knelt to say my prayer, when I heard something under my stand. I glanced down and saw a deer standing under me looking up. The deer ran off when I moved and I started praying again and the deer came back. The deer came by my stand three times while I was praying. When I finished praying the deer left and never came back. I couldn't keep from smiling the rest of the hunt. It was a wonderful and successful hunt even if I didn't get that deer.

One deer season I wasn't going to get to hunt much because of an injury. I was really down in the dumps about not being able to hunt and be out in the woods. One day I was driving down the road when I heard a voice telling me not to worry "you'll get a deer." It scared me at first but then I realized it was God telling me to have faith. When I did get the chance to hunt, I hadn't been in the woods an hour when I killed a nice spike buck. I took a few minutes as I always do to thank God for a wonderful hunt. God is good in taking care of small things and great things!

That same year I was reading some scripture about prayer. "And whatever things you ask in prayer, believing, you will receive." (Matthew 21:22.NKJV) The next time I went hunting and was saying my prayer that Scripture came to mind. I had never asked specifically for a big buck; I usually pray for a safe and successful hunt and a successful hunt for me is just to see some deer. As I was praying I asked God for a good buck.

The morning was beautiful and the forest was alive with wildlife. I sat in my tree stand full of faith and confidence that I was going to get a good buck. At about ten o'clock I looked to my left and saw a nice buck walking down the ridge. I thought he was going to walk away from me before I would be able to get a clear shot. I grabbed my grunt call and made some doe and buck calls. The buck turned and came right toward me. I carefully raised my gun trying not to draw his attention or give away my position. Deer have a keen sense of even the slightest movement. Getting him precisely in my sights I held my breath and steadily pulled the trigger. Before I even walked down to look at the buck I dropped to my knees and thanked the Lord. Every time I look at that eight point rack on my wall I think of the power of prayer and a very successful hunt.

The next and last time I went hunting that year I had another buck walk right under my stand. It was a small buck and I let it walk on by. I had to bite my finger to keep from laughing as the buck walked around under my stand and I thanked the Lord once again for another successful hunt. I told my wife Karla that it shouldn't, but it did scare me to witness the awesome power of prayer. God has answered my prayers and I have seen evidence of His guiding hand many times in my life, but on these hunts I could absolutely feel His presence.

Memories and Miracles

Ask and it will be given to you; seek and you will find; knock and the door will be opened to you. For everyone who asks receives; he who seeks finds; and to him who knocks, the door will be opened.

Matthew 7:7-8 NIV

The Fishing Trip

In the mid-70's I had the privilege of working with a great bunch of men at the Tennessee Forging Steel Mill. The entire shift would make plans weeks ahead for fishing and hunting trips. Sometimes the trip itself wasn't nearly as much fun as the planning had been. One such fishing trip comes to mind with both laughter and fear.

We had planned a walleye fishing trip to Center Hill Lake in Tennessee. We had never been to this particular part of the lake before so it was a great new adventure. I was to pick up a friend and meet the rest of the men at the lake. We went to my Dad's house and got our family boat and made the one-and-a-half-hour trip to the lake. I found the boat ramp and launched the boat. I pulled the truck to the parking area and started walking back to the boat, but before I got to the boat, two snakes fell out of a tree and landed very close to me. I got to the boat in record time, started the motor and headed up the river to meet the other men. Almost as soon as I started out I realized the motor wasn't running right: it would only idle. Dad had failed to mention he had been having trouble with the throttle cable. As we slowly idled toward our destination I was awed by the beauty I saw around me. It was an ideal place to fish, with glorious rock formations and rushing waterfalls. While I was looking for rocks under the shallow water, where fish are often found, I saw several snakes in the low bushes at the waters edge near the bank.

We finally met the other men and started fishing for the elusive walleye. I have always found the walleye very hard to catch but it is one of the best tasting fish in this part of the country. We had been fishing for only a short while when a terrible thunderstorm came up. The lightning was flashing all around and we were fishing from an aluminum boat. Knowing aluminum is a good conductor, we decided to go ashore and wait out the storm. We got out on the shore and you know from an earlier story in this book that I have good reason to be very scared of lightning. Standing there looking down so I wouldn't have to look at the lightning, I noticed several snakes were crawling between our feet. So there I was, standing in the presence of two of my worst fears, snakes and lightning. Except for the incredibly beautiful scenery, that trip ranks number one as the worst trip I have ever taken. The planning was definitely more fun than the reality of that particular fishing expedition.

However, our lives are a lot like that fishing trip. We plan a beautiful life for our children and ourselves, but it doesn't always turn out like we planned. That's the trouble with human plans. They often fail. The one plan you can be sure of, is God's plan. The plan of salvation is the same today and forever.

For by grace you have been saved through faith, and that not of yourselves, it is the gift of God.

                                        Ephesians 2:8 NKJV

Six C's Of Salvation

1. Condition   Romans 9:30-33

2. Confession   Romans 10:9-10

3. Commitment   Romans 10:9

4. Confidence   Romans 10:9

5. Courage   Romans 10:11

6. Consequence   Romans 10:12-13

Memories and Miracles

What shall we say then? That Gentiles who did not pursue righteousness, have attained to righteousness, even the righteousness of faith; But Israel, pursuing the law of righteousness, has not attained to the law of righteousness. Why? Because they did not seek by faith, but as it were, by the works of the law. For they stumbled at that stumbling stone. As it is written, Behold, I lay in Zion a stumbling stone and rock of offense; and whoever believes on Him will not be put to shame."

Romans 9:30-33 NKJV

That if you confess with thy mouth the Lord Jesus and believe in your heart that God has raised him from the dead, you will be saved. For with the heart one believes unto righteousness; and with the mouth confession is made unto salvation. For the scripture saith, Whoever believes on Him will not be put to shame. For there is no distinction between Jew and Greek, for the same Lord over all is rich to all who call upon Him. For whoever calls on the name of the Lord shall be saved.

Romans: 10:9-13 NKJV

Memories and Miracles

The Drive Home

There have been many miracles while driving an automobile, but one comes to mind that could have and should have taken my life except for the grace of God. In the mid-80's, the only employment I could find was two-hundred-forty miles away at a steel mill in Birmingham Alabama. I had been working for the state of Tennessee in a regional prison but it just didn't pay enough for me to provide for my family the way I wanted to. The job in Alabama paid well, but I had to stay there during the week and drive home on my days off. I couldn't afford to move my family, so I rented a house with two other men from Tennessee. The other two men were on a different shift than I was, so I had the house mostly to myself. Being on a different shift also meant I had to make the long trip home by myself. The two times a month I had enough off time to make the Tennessee trip was always either at night or following a night shift. On those long drives it was very difficult to stay awake. The last trip I made from Birmingham was one I made only through God's guiding hand.

I had left the city lights of Birmingham and was on a long stretch of interstate 59 where there was nothing but darkness. As my lights penetrated the night I saw only the white lines and endless highway ahead of me. I have no idea how many miles I had been driving in a mesmerized sleep when I suddenly woke and found myself coming to a sudden stop in the middle of interstate 59.

I will never know how many unseen dangers God protected me from during those miles driven literally while I was asleep. Further down the road I found a church and slept in their parking lot until I was sure I could make it home. Just like during the war, I know God watched over me and guided me home.

I know the plans I have for you," declared the Lord, "Plans to prosper you and not to harm you. Plans to give you a hope and a future

> Jeremiah 29:11 NIV

Memories and Miracles

Memories and Miracles

The Beginning

I have tried to put into this book many of the stories I would have difficulty expressing verbally. I jokingly tell people I am quiet and shy, but in reality I say things I shouldn't. Even when I try to think things out before I say them, they frequently come out all wrong. One of my prayers is to be a better person so that if I can't speak powerfully, at least I can be a good witness through my actions. This a real challenge sometimes.

After writing these stories I realize how naïve and immature I've been over the years. I've been insulated through a close family life and have spent much of my time by myself. Looking back, I wish I had spent more time studying, reading and making new friends. The making new friends was the hard part for me, because I've spent so much time by myself that I have a hard time coming up with enough words to carry on a conversation. Sometimes I stutter and stammer while trying to remember what I'm talking about.

Now that I look back at my experiences in Vietnam I realize I wasn't trained well enough to be a crewmember on a helicopter, but I gave all I had for a country boy who was put in charge of a helicopter and its crew. I think back now at the possibilities of getting shot down and not knowing how to escape, because I didn't have a proper compass or even map reading classes. In the air if you gave me a heading I could get you there, but on the ground I would have been totally lost.

I remember Dad taking us hunting when I was a young boy. We always went to the same places and I knew them like the back of my hand. But I remember a hunt with my cousin that turned out to be a half-day walk trying to find my car, because it was new territory.

In closing, I want to thank all my pilots and crews for the close camaraderie we shared. I could never fully express my appreciation to the special friends I had, and for the promise we made to keep each other out of trouble and away from drugs. I hope that by writing these stories and seeing the love God has for me I can be a better husband, father and grandfather to my wonderful family.

Finally, I hope and pray this book can be my way of being a witness for God. This book also wouldn't be complete without thanks to my wife Karla for standing by me while I've gone through some hard times remembering these events. We've been through some good times and some bad times, but I know our prayers and faith have carried us through. I hope you too will look back at all the wonderful things God has done in your life and if you haven't already, accept Jesus as your Lord and Savior.

Dear Lord, thank you for the strength and wisdom to write this book. Let me be a shining light to help lead others to you. When I get lost or stray, help me that I may use your Word as a compass to guide me back. Amen

In the same way let your light shine before men, that they may see your good deeds and praise your Father in heaven.

Matthew 5:16 NIV

Glossary of Terms

AC: Aircraft Commander - Person in charge of aircraft during flight.

AK-47: Basic assault weapon of the VC

AO: Area of operations

ARVN: Army of the Republic of Vietnam

Autorotation: Emergency landing when a helicopter loses power

C-5: Military cargo aircraft about the same size as a 747 that can carry 70-ton tanks and more

C&C: Command and Control

Chicken plate: Aircrew body armor

Chieu Hoi: A surrender program offered to VC/NVA

Cobra: The AH-1 series of attack helicopters

Collective: The helicopter flight control which makes it rise and descend by adding or decreasing pitch to all rotor blades simultaneously

CO: Commanding Officer

Cyclic: The helicopter flight control, which increases rotor blade pitch to one side while decreasing opposite pitch to cause the aircraft to move in a specific direction.

Door gunner: A solder, usually enlisted, who mans an articulated machine gun on a helicopter

Fire Support Base: Artillery- semi permanent facilities

Gideons: An international non-profit organization of professionals who serve as an extended Missionary arm of the church. This organization primary mission is placing and distributing The Word of God worldwide

Gunship: Certain types of armed aircraft used for ground attack

Hootch: Living quarters

Huey: The UH-1 Iroquois helicopter and all its variants

Insert: To place troops into an area by aircraft

JP-4: Standard turbine aircraft fuel (kerosene base)

KIA: Killed in action

Lam Son 719: A combat operation into Laos from February 8 to April 6, 1971

Loach: Light observation helicopter (LOH)

LRRP: Long- range reconnaissance patrol

LZ: Landing zone

Medevac: Medical evacuation

Mini-gun: A 7.62 mm electric-drive Gatling gun

NVA: North Vietnam Army

Revetment: Earth filled 50-gallon steel drums surrounding a helicopter parking area

Rotor: The spinning wing assembly of a helicopter

RA: Royal Ambassadors is a Bible-centered, church-based, Southern Baptist, mission education organization for boys in grades 1-6

Slick: A huey configured to carry troops

Tracer: A bullet that leaves a bright flash along its flight path

TVA: Tennessee Valley Authority

Important Information

The common belief is that the fighting in Vietnam was not as intense as in World War II.

The average infantryman in the South Pacific during World War II saw about forty days of combat in four years.

The average infantryman in Vietnam saw about Two Hundred and Forty days of combat in one year thanks to the mobility of the helicopter.

One out of every ten Americans who served in Vietnam was a casualty. 58,169 were killed and 304,000 wounded out of 2.59 million who served.

Although the percent that died is similar to other wars, amputations or crippling wounds were 300 percent higher than in World War II.

75,000 Vietnam veterans are severely disabled.

Medevac helicopters flew nearly 500,000 missions. Over 900,000 patients were airlifted (nearly half were Americans).

The average time lapse between wounding to hospitalization was less than one hour. As a result less than one percent of all Americans wounded who survived the first 24 hours died.

Approximately 12,000 helicopters saw action in Vietnam

Army UH-1's totaled 7,531,955 flight hours in Vietnam between October 1966 and the end of 1975.

Source: *Vietnam Helicopter Crew Members Association-by permission*

Memories and Miracles

www.ingramcontent.com/pod-product-compliance
Lightning Source LLC
Chambersburg PA
CBHW021426070526
44577CB00001B/81